the **best** *in*
bridalwear
design

Joy McKenzie

Foreword by Catherine Rayner

B.T. Batsford Ltd • London

Acknowledgements

I would like to thank my family and friends, and also those most directly involved in the production of this publication without whose support it would not have been possible. To Richard Reynolds, Executive Editor and Martina Stansbie, Editor at B.T. Batsford Ltd; Catherine Rayner of Catherine Rayner Ltd; Paul Hammond and Monica Fernandez of R.D. Franks; Carole Hamilton, Editor of *You and Your Wedding*; Leslie Neil, Editor of *Bride and Groom*; Sandra Boler, Editor of *Brides and Setting Up Home*; Carol Spencer, Author of *Wedding Style Counsel*; Rosemary Archer of Berketex Brides Ltd; Annie Harvey of Annie PR Limited; Joanna Dixon of Stephanie Churchill PR Ltd; Colette Mahon, Editor of *Bridal Buyer*; the London College of Fashion Library; the National Art Library and the British Fashion Council.

Dedication

This book is dedicated to my parents Mitchell and Monica McKenzie.

© Joy McKenzie 1998

First published 1998

Printed in Singapore by Kyodo Printing Co.

for the Publisher

B.T. Batsford

583 Fulham Road

London SW6 5BY

ISBN 0 7134 8037 8

A CIP catalogue record for this book is available from the British Library.

Designed by DWN Ltd London.

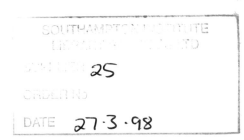

contents

Foreword

Catherine Rayner

Contemporary bridalwear is an anachronism: it is a craft that involves endless care and attention lavished equally on the bride and on the dress. This care and attention derives from an age when more importance was placed on detail and service than on mere commerce. I have never met a designer, nor indeed a bride, who did not care passionately about the tiniest detail of the dress.

Current bridalwear design no longer reflects current fashion trends but sets them – on equal terms with the rest of the industry. The standard of design, the excellence of ideas and the pure innovation of many bridalwear designers have established bridalwear as a couture for the Nineties.

◀ **Catherine Rayner:** 'Café au Lait' dress with a fitted bodice made from silk duchess satin and a taffeta skirt.

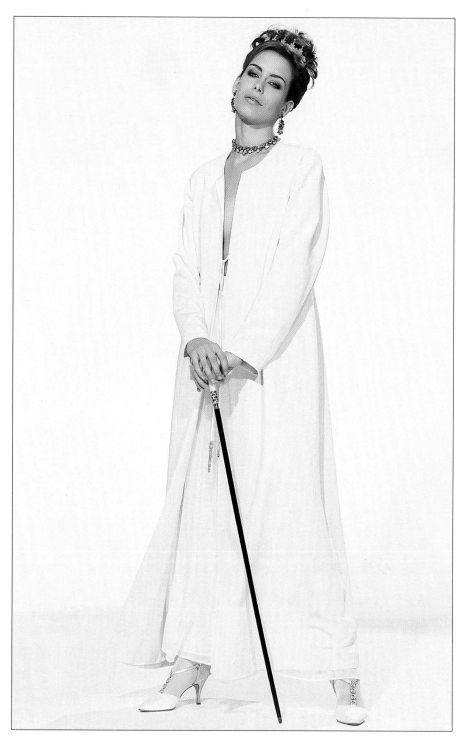

© You and Your Wedding Magazine/Photograph: Iain Philpott.

Introduction

Every wedding dress can be considered a unique masterpiece. The design of each wedding dress is an opportunity to delve into history and to revel in past and present trends and fantasy. A wedding dress must be quite distinctive from all other gowns in order to retain a timeless quality, existing outside fashion, but stylish none the less.

A bridalwear designer must balance the personality of the bride with practical considerations such as fabrics, trimmings, the overall silhouette and design details.

For most women, their bridal dress will probably be the only one that they have custom-made. Hand work is a time-consuming process for which few people are adequately trained. High-quality fabrics are expensive; the design process is lengthy; but if a gown is to be a couture masterpiece there is simply no other way to produce it.

Designers achieve the perfect fit by first cutting a toile, or trial garment, the basic body of the dress; next, there follow two or three fittings. Then the true gown is made, with both an inner and an outer body. The inner body must fit like a glove, with each seam hand-finished. Raw edges are hidden between the inner and outer body. Trimmings (smooth zippers, buttons, hooks and eyes) are sewn by hand. Whatever the style, every gown is perfectly finished on the inside and outside, ensuring the luxury of the bespoke dress.

'Couture' refers to those designers whose work is – literally – at the cutting edge of style. But in 1992, Yves Saint Laurent said that 'Couture will be dead by the year 2000'. Does the future of fashion lie with ready-to-wear, accessible to all? Couturiers design an extravagant bridal gown as a finale to each show; not only as a fantasy extravaganza, but because bridal gowns are the most popular items. Perhaps, then, the bridal business will lead couture into the future.

◀ **Amanda Wakeley:** ivory full-length collarless coat worn with chiffon trousers.

Bridal dresses

The wedding dress incorporates the highest standards of couture workmanship. Brides are more likely than not to opt for a traditional white wedding gown, but this fails to do justice to the options available. Wedding gowns can be ultra-feminine, simply sophisticated or elaborately embroidered, pure white or painted with colour, streamlined or flowing with frills and flounces.

The diversity of choice appears confusing. To simplify the matter, broadly speaking wedding dresses can be divided into two categories: straight dresses and curved dresses. Straight dresses include Grecian and medieval styles, 1920s and 1930s flapper styles, 1960s Empire lines and the natural-looking styles of the 1970s.

Curved dresses include Elizabethan and Victorian styles, Edwardian riding styles and 1940s and 1950s glamour styles – not forgetting the romantic styles of the 1980s. The sheer multitude of styles allows each bride to express her own personal style through her wedding dress.

The ball gown is probably the most popular, as well as being the traditional, bridal dress. It has a full bell-shaped skirt, supported by petticoats or hoops, and a fitted bodice which flatters most figures, accentuating the waist. The many variations come particularly in the design details: the sleeves, necklines, waistlines or trains.

The sheath dress is a less traditional choice. It wraps around the bride's body, creating a revealing, contoured silhouette. Sheaths can be short- or long-skirted and are very often concealed by a detachable train or overskirt. Because they are tight-fitting, sheaths are usually worn without an underskirt or petticoat.

The A-line dress was introduced by Christian Dior, whose garment silhouettes were often named by the letter that embodied the garment's shape. The A-line has a fitted bodice and shoulder straps, but is substantially less restricting than the sheath as the gown flares gracefully from the waistline to the hem. A high-waisted petticoat sits well under the skirt, as it keeps the skirt sturdy and retains the distinctive A-line. This is a flattering style, especially for petite brides, as the elongated skirt presents the illusion of length.

◀ **Kesté:** 'Petruchka' Russian ballerina
dress in pale blue silk chiffon with
hand-painted bodice.

The silhouette of the Empire line dress is a single elegant line, drawn from neoclassical styles. It has a high-waisted skirt which starts immediately under the bust. The bodice can be moulded to support a larger bust or simply left free to give a soft line. Sometimes the bodice is made in a contrasting fabric to the skirt, further emphasizing the high-waisted style. The Princess line is a close relation of the Empire line. The dress is fitted through shoulders and bodice; there is no waistline, but the skirt flares gently outwards.

The suit presents a modern silhouette. It has many potential combinations: a jacket and skirt, perhaps styled as an Edwardian riding jacket with pencil-line skirt; jacket and trousers; or a dress and coat. Considerations when choosing an appropriate suit are, first, the colour, then the shape and finally whether the bride has a straight- or curved-line figure.

The cut of the bridal dress is its foundation: it determines which additional details are selected, such as the sleeves, neckline and train. Each design detail must combine with the line and the fabric to present a harmonious whole.

The neckline is a focal point: people notice it first. The neckline should therefore flatter the bride's face as well as draw attention to the strongest features of her figure. The sweetheart neckline is a classic design. It is low, resembling the rounded curves of a heart, and was first popular in the 1930s and 1940s.

An off-the-shoulder neckline falls below the shoulders, with either a collar or a sleeve resting on the arm. A bodice for an off-the-shoulder gown needs support from boning and/or elastic in its construction. An open neckline often extends off the shoulders.

A portrait collar, or fichu, wraps around the shoulders and is gathered to a point in front, at the bust. The portrait collar is aptly named: it frames and highlights the bride's face and neck. A wedding band collar, popular in the late 19th century, is a high fitted collar.

An illusion neckline is a high neckline with either a wedding band collar or a scoop neck. The bodice is usually see-through and made of sheer net or chiffon. A strapless neckline or a bodice which is sleeveless is usually boned and moulded into the chest and co-ordinates well with a bolero jacket.

▶ **Mori Lee:** dress in satin.

A bateau neckline was popular in the 1950s with French designers. It traces a shallow curve across the collarbone and is out the same front and back. A jewel neckline, originally designed as a background for jewels, consists of a high rounded line, without a collar or binding. The V-neckline is quite simply cut in a V-shape at the back and/or front. Some are deep and extend to the waistline, while others are shallow.

The scoop neckline shows off a beautiful neck and shoulders to perfection as it is a low curve extending to the shoulders. Variations may also sweep deep at the front and/or back.

It is imperative to select the appropriate waistline, as it shapes the dress, bringing proportions to the silhouette.

A natural waistline, as the name implies, sits at the waist and is used with the majority of ball gown wedding dresses. The most popular waistline, however, is the basque, quite simply because it looks good on anyone. It sits at the natural waistline, but dips to a lower point in the front, usually describing a V-line. This gives the impression of a very slim waist.

There are just as many sleeves as there are necklines. Sleeves can be divided into two categories: short or long.

Short sleeves include the puff sleeve, which is gathered at the armhole, the cuff or the band of the sleeve and which ends just below the elbow. A cap sleeve covers the top of the arm; a three-quarter sleeve ends just below the elbow and is often finished with a small band or cuff.

There are at least as many long sleeves as short ones. The Juliette sleeve has a short puff at the shoulder but is a long fitted sleeve named after the Shakespearean heroine. The bishop's sleeve is a full long sleeve gathered at the wrist. The leg-o-mutton sleeve, or gigot, is wide and exaggerated, rounded at the shoulders and tapering to fit the lower arm. A fitted sleeve is long and narrow, with either a row of buttons at the wrist or a single button or snap fastening.

Trains date back to the Middle Ages, when they were an indication of the wearer's rank. Today the train indicates the formality of a wedding and the respect paid to tradition.

◀ **Suzanne Neville:** fitted silk crepe dress with ruched satin waist and train.

© Bride and Groom Magazine/Photograph: Chris Lane/Suzanne Neville.

Chapel or cathedral trains are suitable for formal or very formal weddings. A chapel train usually extends for about one metre; a cathedral train is one that extends to any length beyond that.

Watteau and court trains, which fall from the shoulders, are less common. The Watteau train is named after Jean Antoine Watteau whose early 18th-century paintings depict women wearing elegant gowns with distinctive pleats. The court train is a separate piece of fabric attached to the shoulders of the gown, and provides a regal tone.

The detachable train is both classic and versatile. It is usually attached at the back of the waist with hooks or buttons. Sometimes it is attached around the circumference of the waist, covering a skirt, and once it is removed a wholly new look is revealed.

▶ **Neil Cunningham:** 'Isis' crepe fishtail dress in cream with draped neckline and tails. Photograph: Anthony Crickmay.

▲ **Short Stories:** (L to R) dresses in
crepe and organza and crepe.

▲ **Short Stories:** crepe, guipure and
chiffon dress.

▼ **Hilary Morgan:** embroidered satin gowns with detachable train.

▲ **Hilary Morgan:** embroidered satin gown.

▲ **Berketex Brides:** full-skirted
sleeveless gown with silk jacquard
panelled bodice and lace back detail.

Berketex

▼ **Berketex Brides:** full-skirted off-the-shoulder gown with organza overskirt.

◀ **Helen Marina:** 'Tripole' satin straight bridal dress with a plunging back 'V' showing lace-up detail and a draped bow.

▲ **Helen Marina:** 'Imogen' bridal gown in ivory silk dupion with train, shaped neckline and waist edged with guipure motifs.

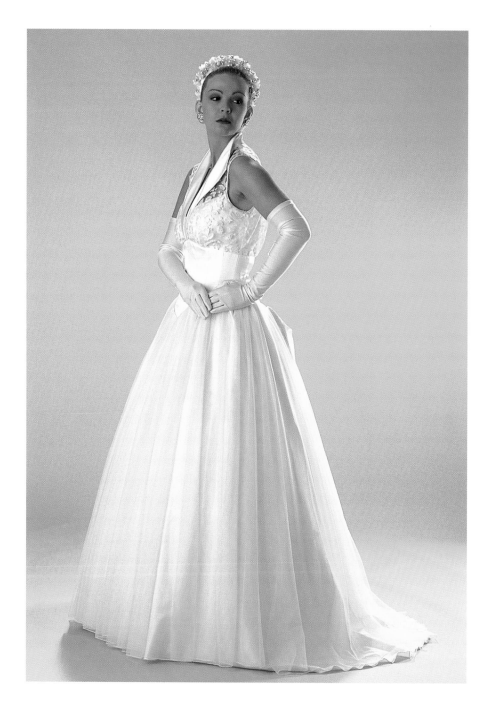

▲ **Sposa Bella:** 'Henrietta' 1950s
style dress with embroidered tulle
bodice, satin collar and tulled skirt.

▲ **Sposa Bella:** 'Olwen' crepe
dress with a beaded bodice and
chiffon sleeves.

Frank Usher

▲ **Frank Usher:** suit-dress made
from raised lace line satin and trimmed
satin with a satin jacket.

▶ **Frank Usher:** suit made from
cotton and polyester.

© You and Your Wedding Magazine/Photograph: Iain Philpott.

▲ **Lila Lace:** pale blue duchess satin
gown with a very long train and pearl
neckline.

◀ **Lila Lace:** 'Twilight' in silver
fortuny tissue and silk satin with scarf.

© Bride and Groom Magazine/Photograph: Malcolm Willison/Lila Lace.

31

▲ **Donna Salado:** 'Lulu' satin
marquise silk dress with beaded lace.

▲ **Donna Salado:** 'Sadie' dress in
acetate and lurex brocade.

▲ **Tracy Connop:** 'Atlanta' dress with sleeveless fitted bodice of beaded French lace and a full gathered skirt in ivory silk.

◀ **Tracy Connop:** 'Franchesca' dress with fitted silk bodice, halter neck strap with chiffon and silk rose detail, gathered front and a long train.

▲ **Brides International:** full-skirted
gown with a rich velvet long-sleeved
bodice and delicate embroidery.

▲ **Brides International:** straight off-the-shoulder gown in duchess satin with train.

▲ **Catherine Davighi:** 'Argenta'
dress with silk corset bodice,
embroidered in silver thread with
pearls and crystals, and circular cut
silk organza skirt with silk underskirt
and full nets.

▲ **Catherine Davighi:** 'Chlöe' dress
in chinese silk dupion with a corset
bodice with silver embroidered panels
and straight skirt with detachable train.

▲ **Mori Lee:** matt satin dress.

▶ **Mori Lee:** satin and lace bridal gown.

Bridal dresses

▼ **The Dress Gallery:** 'Jade' heavily-boned duchess silk bodice with a hand embroidered and beaded bouquet of roses, caught with a satin bow.

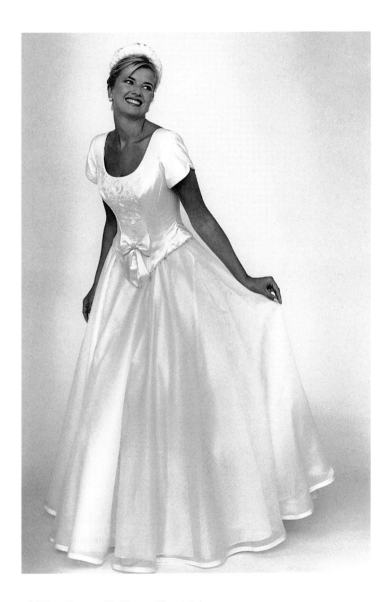

◄ **The Dress Gallery:** 'Patricia' empire line dress with corded lace bodice.

▲ **Short Stories:** dress in a brocade
fabric.

▲ **Short Stories:** dress in crepe and chiffon.

▲ **Jo Ann Hall:** 'Symphony' princess line dress in champagne silk crepe, with a gold bodice and silk duchess satin braids.

▶ **Jo Ann Hall:** 'Adelaide' shoestring strapped gown with godet train in ivory microfibre. The cropped 'Portia' bolero is made in guipure lace.

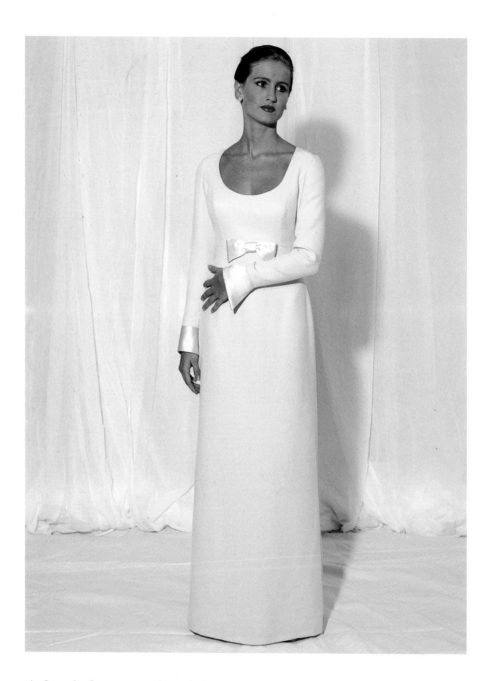

▲ **Angela Stone:** straight-styled
dress with fitted sleeves in satin
backed crepe.

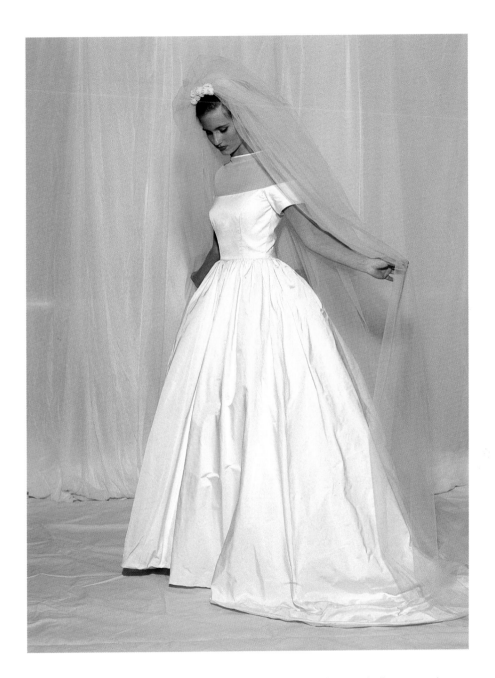

▲ **Angela Stone:** ball-gown style dress in silk duchess satin and silk georgette.

▼ **Suzanne Glenton:** 'Audrey'
duchess satin square neck sheath and
matching jacket.

◀ **Suzanne Glenton:** 'Audrey'
square neck sheath dress with front
dart detail in ivory silk duchess satin.

▲ **Hilary Morgan:** silk off-the-shoulder gown (left) and satin and chiffon off-the-shoulder gown (right).

▼ **Hilary Morgan:** embroidered satin gown.

▲ **Phillipa Lepley:** 'Goldilocks' full-skirted satin brocade dress.

▶ **Phillipa Lepley:** 'Sandra' beaded duchess satin princess line dress.

▼ **Jo-Ann Crossfield:** 'Midnight Navy' full-length velvet hooded coat with georgette detail worn over navy dress with velvet bodice and silk skirt.

© Bride and Groom Magazine/Photograph: Alex James/Jo-Ann Crossfield.

▼ **Bride & Gowns:** 'Yvette' in crushed fur trimmed velvet with matching cape.

© Bride and Groom Magazine / Photograph: Alex James / Bride & Gowns.

▲ **Ritva Westenius:** 'Laurel' double crepe dress with cowl neckline.

◄ **Ritva Westenius:** 'Alexandra' dress with hand-embroidered silk dupion corset bodice beaded with pearls.

▲ **Andrea Wilkin:** long-sleeved
dress.

▶ **Ritva Westenius:** 'Lady Richmond'
dress.

▼ **Neil Cunningham:** 'Agnes' silver
duchess satin empire line dress with
crystal beaded cropped jacket and full
train. Photograph: Anthony Crickmay.

▶ **Neil Cunningham:** 'All Smiles'
duchess satin sheath with trapeze line
organza overlay and flat satin bows on
the shoulder. Photograph: Anthony
Crickmay.

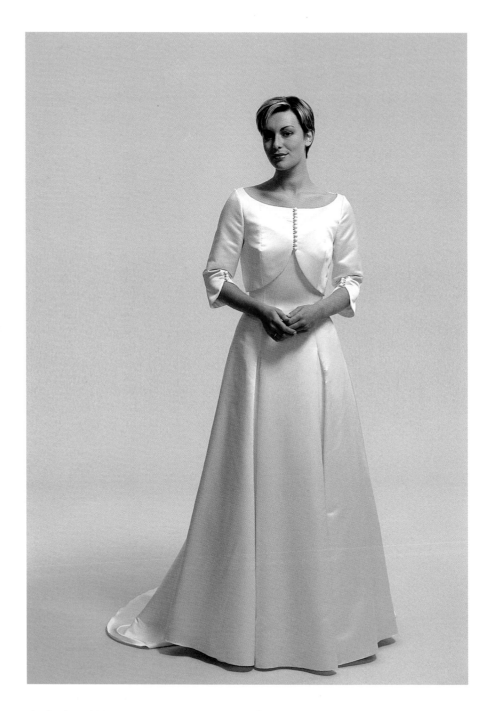

▲ **Andrea Wilkin:** duchess satin A-line dress with matching bolero jacket.

▶ **Andrea Wilkin:** dress with silk mille feuille bodice and toffee silk skirt.

▼ **Basia Zarzycka:** 'My Dearest
Emma' wedding gown in grand silk
duchess satin with lamé chantilly lace.

◄ **Basia Zarzycka:** 'Wild Rose
Collection' long shift duchess satin
gown, overlaid with long frock coat in
chantilly lace, and tudor rose chapeau.
Photograph: Massimo Marino.

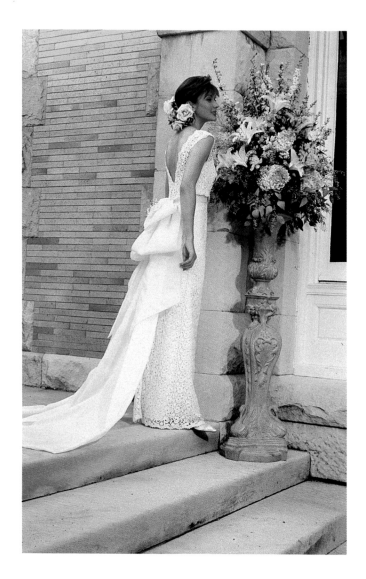

▲ **Alfred Angelo:** slim-fitting
sleeveless dress with curved sabrina
neckline, organza slashed waist and
large streamed bow.

▼ **Caroline Parkes:** light blue
duchess satin sheath dress with bow,
front train and sequinned silk chiffon top.

© You and Your Wedding Magazine/Photograph: Iain Philpott.

▼ **Short Stories:** guipure and
duchess satin dress.

▲ **Short Stories:** crepe and guipure
dresses.

▼ **Berketex Brides:** full-skirted
duchess satin gown with sweetheart
neckline.

▲ **Berketex Brides:** full-skirted silk
gown with long sleeves.

▼ **Zandra Rhodes:** dress with gold-and-white lace bodice with hand made silk chiffon roses around the neckline and white tulle skirt with a gold-and-white silk chiffon overskirt designed to be pulled up for a tiered effect. Photograph: Rose Beddington.

▶ **Zandra Rhodes:** punk wedding dress with acetate bosom band and rayon jersey skirt. Photograph: Clive Arrowsmith.

74

▲ **Gillian Leavy:** 'All Wrapped Up',
inspired by the 1920s flappers, made
from pure silk faille.

▲ **The House of Nicholas:** handbeaded duchess satin dress, sleeves and train in georgette.

▼ **Hilary Morgan:** silk embroidered
lace gown with lace back detail.

◀ **Hilary Morgan:** satin and organza
gown.

▲ **Sposa Bella:** French macramé lace
bodice with crepe skirt.

◀ **Sposa Bella:** 'Bali Hai' paradise
beach wedding outfit with macramé
lace crop top and miniskirt worn with
crepe sarong.

© You and Your Wedding Magazine/Photograph: Chris Lane.

▲ **Louise:** short ivory A-line sheath
with chiffon overdress.

▶ **Diva Bridalwear:** ivory crushed
velvet gown with corset bodice,
trimmed with ostrich feathers.

© Bride and Groom Magazine/Photograph: Chris
Lane/Diva Bridalwear.

▼ **Lila Lace:** ice blue duchess satin dress with ruched waist line and full train.

© Bride and Groom Magazine/Photograph: Janine Wilkes/Lila Lace.

▲ **Kesté:** 'Can-Can' white broderie anglaise gown with suede corset and skirt with 12 pure cotton petticoats.

Kesté

© Bride and Groom Magazine/Photograph: Philip North Coombes/Two's Company.

▲ **Two's Company:** red embroidered dupion silk dress with detachable train.

◀ **The Design Room:** velvet off-the-shoulder bodice with embroidery and pink duchess satin skirt.

© You and Your Wedding Magazine/Photograph: Iain Philpott.

▼ **Alan Hannah:** 'Arletta' duchess
satin dress with hand beaded bodice.

▶ **SoieMeme:** richly pearly-beaded
shift dress with side split.

© Bride and Groom Magazine/Photograph: Janine Wilkes/SoieMeme.

Tracy Connop

▲ **Tracy Connop:** 'Beatrice' straight-shaped dress in Italian appliquéd fabric with a chiffon background and a long train in pure silk.

◄ **Suzanne Neville:** empire line dress with a silk duchess satin bodice and train and a silk crepe skirt.

▼ **Lyndsay Hepburn:** 'Louise'
halter-neck gown in ivory Thai silk and
tulle with ruched waist, pearl detailing
and detachable train.

© Bride and Groom Magazine/Photograph: Tim Winter/Lyndsay Hepburn.

▶ **David Fielden:** gown with chiffon
bodice and overskirt and a huge bow
detail on an empire-line skirt.

© You and Your Wedding Magazine/Photograph:
Rod Nissen-Petzer.

▲ **Short Stories:** crepe guipure and
chiffon dress

▶ **Suzanne Glenton:** 'Leva'
buttercup duchess satin strapless gown
with hip sash.

© Bride and Groom Magazine/Photograph: Alex
James/Suzanne Glenton.

▼ **Phillipa Lepley:** 'Oyster Sache'
duchess satin bodice with silk organza
skirt.

▶ **Catherine Rayner:** 'Lilly' sheath
bridal dress with fitted bodice and a
flowing skirt in silk duchess satin.

▲ **Jenny Tyler:** flapper-style sheath dress from two ply Thai
silk overlaid with chantilly lace, with deep lace ruffles around
the cuffs and soft chiffon bows. The dress has a low 'V' back
with chiffon swathed around the waist, which ties in a bow
with long trails at the back and is fnished with a two ply Thai
train, with a pearl cabochon at the front of the waist.

▶ **Sarah Whitworth:** pink satin
corset dress with bustle.

© You and Your Wedding Magazine/Photograph: Chris Lane.

▼ **Amanda Wakeley:** ivory mikado silk strapless A-line dress.

Amanda Wakeley

© You and Your Wedding Magazine/Photograph: John Bishop.

▶ **Jenny Tyler:** 'Madrigal' dress in cotton damask with hat and muff.

© Bride and Groom Magazine/Photograph: Chris Lane/Jenny Tyler.

▲ **Abe Hamilton:** crushed silk dress with flower appliqué.

▶ **Jo Ann Hall:** 'Venice' empire line silk crepe gown with sweetheart neckline, and pearl detail on bodice line and sleeves.

© Bride and Groom Magazine/Photograph: Steve Maddox/Jane Baker

▲ **Jane Baker:** ivory duchess satin sheath dress with a silk organza opera coat.

▶ **Angela Stone:** crepe dress with pearl trimmed neckline and cut-out detail.

© You and Your Wedding Magazine/Photograph: Howard Daniels.

◀ **Kesté:** Celtic style coat in silk organza with embroidered cuff neckline and edge of coat; pale green silk crepe dechine overlaid with an ivory embroidered chiffon bodice beaded with crystals and silver.

▲ **Mori Lee:** tulle skirt with beaded
lace bodice.

▶ **Tomasz Starzewski:** hand-beaded stretch lycra tulle bodice mounted on a strapless corset with lavishly embroidered silk, tulle over silk ziberline skirt.

▲ **Tomasz Starzewski:** hand-beaded silk ziberline hooded frock coat with pom-pom trim.

▲ **Short Stories:** dress in crepe, lace and chiffon.

▼ **Rena Koh:** 'Chantal' dress.

Bridal accessories

When considering hats and headdresses, the shape, style and fit are each crucial.

Hats are not worn as frequently today as they were in the past. Consequently many women no longer wear them with confidence. However, when chosen with care, a hat can be the perfect match for any wedding dress.

Angular hats have square crowns and flat brims, are generally made with stiff fabrics and are finished with Petersham Trim and sturdy decorations. Curved hats have softer features, such as rounded crowns and floppy brims, and are usually made of more pliable materials and are accompanied with lace or floral trimmings.

When choosing a headdress, the shape of the bride's face is the essential factor.

A woman with an oval face-shape has the freedom to experiment with most headdresses and hairstyles. If the bride is tall, she could try a style with a great deal of width, choosing a headdress made from stiff nylon rather than drapery silk or lace veils. Conversely, a petite bride with this face type might wish to employ a hairstyle or headdress that adds height to her head.

A heart-shaped face should not add extra width at the top. If the bride has short hair, a short veil with much width at the shoulders is an ideal choice. By contrast, a pear-shaped head is shown off to best advantage when the hair is kept minimal at chin-level but is full at the forehead.

For a round face, choose a style with some height that will simultaneously lengthen and slim the face. If the bride has long hair, it will look splendid up.

Hair can either be taken back or kept short for a diamond-shaped face; voluminous hair, or a headdress, at the forehead will also suit.

A rectangular face will benefit from a fringe or headdress; a bride with a square-shaped face might try an off-the-face hairstyle.

Floral wreaths can be worn over the forehead or nestled in the hair. The Juliet cap is a headdress that fits tightly to the crown of the head and is made entirely of pearls

▲ **Rachel Trevor-Morgan:** hat made from burnt ostrich feather puffs.

or jewels. A mantilla is a large veil which surrounds the face. A 'profile' is a decorative comb worn on one side of the head, silhouetting the face. A tiara, a crown resting on top of the head, is a graceful and classic choice.

Veils are – technically – another type of headdress. The ballet veil, also known as a waltz, comes to just an inch above the floor. A bird cage veil is made of stiff material, covers the face and falls to just below the chin. A blusher veil is loose, and is worn forward over the bride's face or lifted back over the headdress. The flyaway veil has multiple layers; in length, it just brushes the shoulders. A fingertip veil is probably the most popular style: it reaches to the fingertips, and like the cathedral veil is suitable for highly formal weddings. A chapel veil falls 2.5 metres from the headdress and suits a formal wedding dress. A cathedral veil falls 3.5 metres from the headdress and is an appropriate complement to a highly formal wedding gown.

Bridal hosiery must match the wedding dress in colour as closely as possible. Choice of hosiery is particularly important if the wedding dress is short. If the dress is white, ivory hosiery may look 'dirty' in comparison. If the dress is ivory, white hosiery will stand out too. If the wedding dress is dark, hosiery can blend rather than having to match exactly.

Hosiery is available in all the bridal shades, including white, ivory, pale pink and blue, and extending to glittering gold and silver as well as florals.

Shoes must be comfortable as well as complementary. Elements to consider include style, colour and heel height: very high heels are not recommended unless a bride is very confident in them.

There are many wedding style specialists who will decorate brides' and bridesmaids' shoes to match or complement dresses and harmonize with flowers or dress decorations.

A shoe style must be chosen to complement the dress. Flat pumps or slippers are ideal for themed or historical dresses and also suit wide-skirted dresses. Sling-back shoes look great with 1950s- and 1960s-style dresses, and are often available with pearl or crystal trim. Dolly shoes (side-buttoned) and T-bar (buckled) shoes both suit 1920s- and 1930s-style dresses; these can be found in silk and satin, and with pearl button fastenings.

High-heeled shoes are suitable for glamorous, figure-hugging 1940s-style dresses.

▲ **Hanna Goldman:** dusky pink
embroidered fabric shoes, melted ink
water for effect, Thai silk, decorated
with pearls and gold beads.

▲ **Jenny Tyler:** skull cap covered with two ply Thai and chantilly lace, encrusted with pearls, antique crystals and bugle beads which are glued to form the beaded fringe.

High-fronted shoes, the fronts often embroidered with curvy, spool-shaped designs, usually have chunky heels at the back. These are ideal for larger feet and thicker ankles and are comfortable to wear. Laced ankle- or calf-length boots in leather or fabric are the perfect option for Edwardian- or Victorian-inspired wedding dresses. Some are side-buttoned, while others lace up: both provide an authentic period touch.

▲ **Short Stories:** brocade dress and hat.

◀ **Hilary Morgan:** silk brocade gown with veil.

▲ **Hanna Goldman:** silk dupion
shoes with gold and ivory pearls and
flowers made from soft organza.

 **Hanna Goldman:** silk shoes.

▲ **Malcolm Morris:** Victorian tiara
with Neptune shells; ivy tiara
handmade in a base metal; tiara plated
with 24 carat gold with Austrian
crystals and glass pearls.

▲ **Josie Baird:** 'Julia' tiara.

▼ **Josie Baird:** 'Julia' opened out as a brooch and earrings.

▲ **Basia Zarzycka:** riding hat in silk
florentine brocade.

▶ **Basia Zarzycka:** tiaras.
Photograph: Massimo Marino.

Index

▲ **Catherine Rayner:** 'Full finale'.

the **best** *in*

bridalwear

design